Recipes FOR CHANGE

Written by
Michael Platt

Illustrated by
Alleanna Harris

MAGIC CAT PUBLISHING

NEW YORK

Contents

Safety Note: Cooking is great fun, but frying, sharp knives, hot stoves, and other elements of cooking can be dangerous. Always have an adult around you while you cook to supervise and assist as needed.

Dear Reader,

I have a strong pride and appreciation for my culture. Resilient, courageous, and diverse, Black leaders and changemakers of the past and present inspire me every day, and with every challenge we have overcome, something has sustained us:

Food.

Food plays—and has played—a vital role in strengthening and shaping Black empowerment. For centuries, we have used food to feed our families, friends, and communities; to celebrate our achievements; and to remember and respect how far we've come. From civil rights activism of the past to the Black Lives Matter movement of today, food continues to empower us.

In this book, I retell the stories of twelve momentous months in Black history to honor the relationship that food and protests have always had, and then share one of my own recipes inspired by these events. I hope this book encourages you to tell your story, share your recipes, and feel empowered, too.

Michael Platt
Food justice advocate and baker

January

It was a cold January morning in Oakland, California, when Huey and Bobby first opened a church's doors to provide a free breakfast to school children.

In October 1966, they had founded the Black Panther Party, a movement to empower Black people across America who were suffering from inequality. The Black Panthers knew that food affects a child's education, and so every morning they served milk, toast, eggs, bacon, and creamy grits to the young people who needed it most.

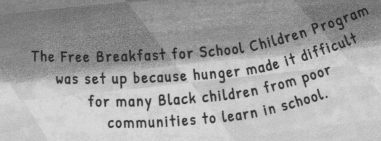

The Free Breakfast for School Children Program was set up because hunger made it difficult for many Black children from poor communities to learn in school.

4

The Black Panthers introduced the program in other cities. By the end of the first year, they had served breakfast to twenty thousand children across the country.

Huey P. Newton and Bobby Seale

Year: 1969

The Black Panther Party's creamy grits

Serves 4

- ¾ cup (110 g) grits, fine cornmeal, maize meal, or instant polenta
- 3 cups (700 ml) milk
- salt, for seasoning
- ¼ cup (55 g) light brown sugar
- 1 tablespoon heavy cream
- butter, for topping

- Place the grits, cornmeal, and maize meal or polenta in a saucepan.

- Pour in the milk and add a pinch of salt. Cook, stirring continuously, over medium heat for approximately 5 minutes, or until the mixture begins to thicken.

- Remove from the heat and stir in the brown sugar and cream.

- Top with butter and serve immediately.

FREE BREAKFAST FOR CHILDREN served here every school-day morning

February

On the first day of February 1960, Ezell, Franklin, Joseph, and David walked into the Woolworth store in Greensboro, North Carolina, and sat down at the "Whites Only" lunch counter.

They ordered slices of cherry pie, but the young men were refused service as the store only served Black customers at the stand-up counter. But they did not move, sitting peacefully until closing time. They returned over the next several days with more supporters. Their quiet act of rebellion sparked sit-ins across the South that helped end racial segregation.

WHITES ONLY

During this time, Black people were kept apart from white people in some places in the United States. This was especially common in the South.

Ezell Blair, Jr., Franklin McCain, Joseph McNeil, and David Richmond
Year: 1960

Thanks to the Greensboro Four, the Woolworth store began serving Black people at its lunch counter in July 1960. Four years later, the Civil Rights Act of 1964 made it against the law to segregate based on skin color.

CHERRY PIE

The Greensboro Sit-In's cherry protest pie

Serves 8

- 2 ready-to-bake pie crusts
- 2 cups (440 g) canned pitted cherries, drained
- 1 cup (200 g) superfine sugar
- finely grated zest of 2 lemons

- 3 tablespoons cornstarch
- ½ teaspoon cinnamon
- ½ teaspoon almond extract
- pinch of nutmeg
- 1 egg, lightly beaten
- 1 tablespoon sugar, for dusting

- Preheat the oven to 400°F (200°C) and grease a 9-inch (23-cm) pie plate. Put a baking sheet in the oven to heat up.

- Unroll one of the pie crusts and line the pie dish, trimming off any excess.

- Line the top of the pie crust with parchment paper and add pie weights to hold it down. Bake for 15 minutes, then carefully remove the paper and weights and cook the pastry for 5 more minutes, or until golden.

- Mix together the rest of the ingredients and pour them into the pie plate.

- Roll out the remaining pie crust and cut into long strips. Weave the strips together over the pie to form a lattice. Press down the edges to seal and trim off any excess. Brush with the beaten egg and sprinkle with sugar.

- Bake for 40 minutes, or until crisp and golden.

- Cool for 20 minutes before serving.

March

Arm in arm, Martin, John, and Hosea led demonstrators on a march for fair voting rights in Selma, Alabama.

Around six hundred marchers reached the edge of Selma on March 7, 1965, when they were attacked by state troopers and local police. The day became known as "Bloody Sunday." Two days later, on "Turnaround Tuesday," they reached the Edmund Pettus Bridge again but turned around to await a court ruling. On March 21, they finally crossed over the Edmund Pettus Bridge, reaching the state capital, Montgomery, three days later. The marches raised awareness of the difficulties faced by Black voters and the need for national action.

At the time, Black people were legally allowed to vote, but officials made it very difficult for them to do so.

As a result of the three marches, President Lyndon B. Johnson signed the Voting Rights Act of 1965, which made it against the law to prevent Black people from voting.

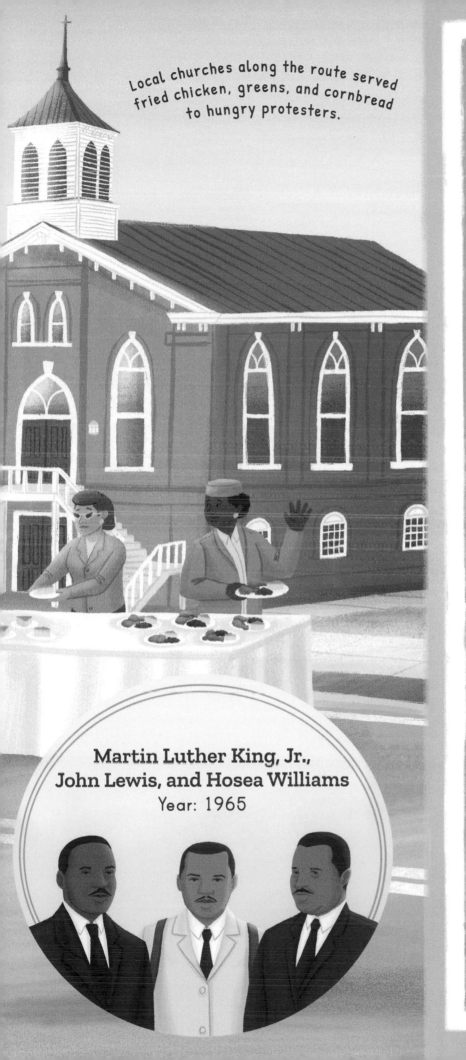

Local churches along the route served fried chicken, greens, and cornbread to hungry protesters.

Martin Luther King, Jr., John Lewis, and Hosea Williams
Year: 1965

The Selma March's carry-on cornbread

Serves 6

- ¼ cup (55 g) butter
- 1 cup (150 g) fine cornmeal
- 1 cup (140 g) all-purpose flour
- 1 tablespoon superfine sugar
- 2 teaspoons baking powder
- 1½ teaspoons salt
- 2¼ cups (570 ml) buttermilk
- 2 large eggs

- Preheat the oven to 425°F (220°C) and grease a 9-inch (23-cm) round cake pan.

- Place the butter in a saucepan. Cook over low heat until the butter is melted, stirring occasionally with a wooden spoon.

- Put all the dry ingredients into a large mixing bowl. Beat the buttermilk and eggs in a separate bowl, then stir in the butter.

- Add the liquid to the dry ingredients and mix together.

- Pour the batter into the cake pan and smooth out the top. Bake for 25 minutes until golden brown.

- Cool for 10 minutes, then remove from pan. Cut into wedges to serve. It's a great accompaniment to fried chicken and braised greens.

April

Throughout the seventeenth and eighteenth centuries, Black people were taken from Africa and forced into slavery in America, mainly on Southern plantations.

In the dead of night, "conductor" Harriet led a group of runaway enslaved people from slavery in Maryland to freedom.

The route they took was called the Underground Railroad, and Harriet knew it well, having escaped slavery that way herself. It wasn't a real railroad but a series of secret safe houses called "stations" that hid enslaved people as they escaped to places where slavery was illegal. Harriet guided the group through the darkness, traveling through woods and foraging for food. After they ate, they followed the North Star until they found their next station: a safe place to eat and sleep when morning's light arrived.

As a conductor, Harriet was responsible for finding food and used her knowledge of the land to forage and fish.

Harriet Tubman
Years: 1850–60

The Underground Railroad's freedom fish

Serves 4

- 8 whiting fillets, skin on
- salt and pepper, for seasoning
- 1½ cups (225 g) fine cornmeal
- 1 tablespoon granulated garlic
- 2 teaspoons salt
- 1 teaspoon pepper
- 1½ cups (350 ml) milk
- 3 tablespoons canola oil
- lemon wedges, for serving

- Season each fish fillet with salt and pepper to taste. Chill in the refrigerator for an hour.

- Mix the cornmeal with the granulated garlic, salt, and pepper in a shallow bowl and set aside. Pour the milk into a second shallow bowl.

- Dip each fillet into the milk, then in the seasoned mix, covering it completely.

- Pour the oil into a non-stick frying pan over medium-high heat.

- Once the pan is hot, place one fillet in the pan, skin-side down. Cook for 3 minutes, or until it is a nice golden color. Carefully turn the fish over and cook for another 2 minutes.

- Remove the fish and let it cool slightly on a wire rack with paper towels underneath.

- Serve warm with a lemon wedge. Whiting is a delicately flavored fish, so it's extra tasty with hot sauce!

May

As a pot of gumbo simmered on the stove, chef Leah looked on at the students gathered in her restaurant.

They were known as Freedom Riders: Black American and white civil rights activists who rode buses together into Southern states to protest against segregated bus terminals. Leah's restaurant, Dooky Chase's, was a secret meeting place for civil rights activists when they came to New Orleans, Louisiana, and provided them with a safe place in which to plan their next protest.

Leah helped to mend the country's divisions one meal at a time. She once said, "We changed the course of America over a bowl of gumbo."

Leah Chase
Year: 1961

The Freedom Rides began in May 1961, and by the fall of that same year, the federal government declared that segregation was not allowed in interstate terminals.

The Freedom Riders' gumbo

Serves 6

- 3 tablespoons canola oil
- 4 andouille sausages, chopped
- ¼ cup (35 g) all-purpose flour
- ½ cup (130 g) tomato paste
- 3 onions, diced
- 1 carrot, diced
- 4 green peppers, diced
- 3 celery sticks, diced
- 6 cups (1.4 l) chicken stock

- 4 tablespoons tomato purée
- 2–3 tablespoons Creole or Cajun seasoning
- 3 garlic cloves, crushed
- 6 thyme sprigs
- 1 bay leaf
- 8 okra pods, cut into half-inch (1.5-cm) circles
- 2 cups (450 g) raw shrimp, defrosted if frozen

- Heat the oil in a heavy-bottomed pot, add the sausages, and fry for a few minutes until browned. Remove and set aside.

- Add the flour to the oil and stir continuously over medium heat until the mixture browns.

- Turn the heat down slightly, add the tomato paste, and cook for 2 minutes. Then add the onions, carrot, peppers, and celery, and cook until just soft.

- Pour in the chicken stock. Then stir in the tomato purée, seasoning, garlic, thyme, bay leaf, and browned sausage. Simmer for an hour, or until the liquid is reduced by half.

- Add the okra and shrimp and simmer for 5 minutes, or until the shrimp are cooked.

- Serve hot. It's delicious over buttery rice.

Walking about three hundred miles of the journey, 89-year-old Opal Lee traveled from Texas to Washington, D.C., to campaign for Juneteenth to be a national holiday.

Juneteenth commemorates June 19, 1865, the day when troops came to Texas to announce the end of slavery. Although slavery should have ended more than two years earlier due to the Emancipation Proclamation, it continued in some places. Juneteenth celebrations live on, and one common way to mark the occasion is through eating red foods, from red ice pops to red velvet cake.

"Even though there's still much work to be done, we have to celebrate the freedom that we have," Opal said. "That's what Juneteenth is about: celebrating freedom each step of the way."

Opal Lee
Year: 2016

In June 2021, President Joe Biden officially made Juneteenth a national holiday, signing the bill into law with Opal by his side.

Juneteenth's red ice pops

Serves 12

- ¼ cup (50 g) superfine sugar
- 4 tablespoons (60 ml) water
- 1 cup (250 g) strawberries
- 1 watermelon, about 5 pounds (2.25 kg)

You will also need:
- popsicle molds
- popsicle sticks

- Put the sugar and water into a saucepan over medium heat. Stir until the sugar has completely dissolved, then set the mixture aside to cool.

- Remove the strawberry leaves and purée the fruit using a blender or food processor. Strain the purée and set aside.

- Cut open your watermelon and scoop the flesh out into a bowl. Pick out any black seeds. Purée the flesh using a blender or food processor, then mix with the puréed strawberries and cooled syrup.

- Insert the sticks into the popsicle molds or paper cups and then pour in the mixture. Freeze for 6 hours, or until set.

- In hot weather, cool down with these refreshing popsicles.

July

Standing in their kitchens in Washington, D.C., chefs Willa, Rob, and Paola appealed for action.

"Calling all bakers, chefs, home bakers, and cooks," they wrote on social media. "We are armed to fight racism with the tools we know how to utilize: our FOOD." Naming their movement Bakers Against Racism, they organized a worldwide virtual bake sale to raise money for Black Lives Matter. Their goal was to recruit eighty bakers, but an incredible two thousand pastry chefs and home bakers joined in to make both sweet and savory food and raised over a million dollars!

Seven years earlier, in July 2013, the Black Lives Matter movement was founded in response to a crime watch volunteer being found not guilty in the fatal shooting of Black teenager Trayvon Martin. Then, in 2020, the death of George Floyd at the hands of a police officer placed a renewed focus on anti-Black racism.

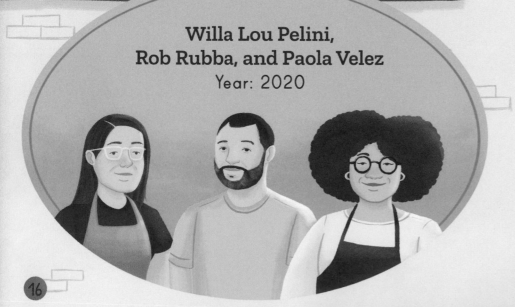

Willa Lou Pelini, Rob Rubba, and Paola Velez
Year: 2020

Black Lives Matter can refer to a hashtag, an anthem, a slogan, or a social movement, all campaigning for racial justice.

Bakers Against Racism's sweet potato hand pie

Serves 8

- 1¼ pounds (600 g) sweet potatoes
- ½ cup (110 g) light brown sugar
- 1 teaspoon cinnamon
- 1 teaspoon nutmeg
- 1 tablespoon heavy cream
- ¼ cup (55 g) butter, melted
- 2 ready-to-bake pie crusts
- 3 cups (710 ml) canola oil
- 2 tablespoons powdered sugar
- 1 teaspoon warm water

- Preheat the oven to 400°F (200°C). Roast the potatoes until soft, then let them cool.

- Scoop the potato flesh into a bowl and mix in the brown sugar, cinnamon, nutmeg, heavy cream, and melted butter.

- Using a 5-inch (12-cm) round cookie cutter, cut out 16 large circles from the pie dough. Place a tablespoon of filling on one half of each circle, fold over, and use a fork to seal the edges.

- Heat the canola oil to 350°F (180°C) in a deep-sided pan. One at a time, carefully add each pie and fry for 4 minutes or until golden brown. Alternatively, brush with melted butter and bake in the oven at 400°F (200°C) for 15 minutes.

- While they cool, make the glaze by mixing the powdered sugar and warm water in a bowl.

- Once the pies have cooled completely, drizzle them with the glaze and serve.

August

Looking out from the Lincoln Memorial in Washington, D.C., Martin saw thousands of supporters who had gathered to hear his speech.

He started slowly, talking about what it was like to be Black in America in 1963 and the racism that still took place a hundred years after the Emancipation Proclamation. His voice then turned to hope: "I have a dream," he declared, "that my four little children will one day live in a nation where they will not be judged by the color of their skin but by the content of their character," and he urged America to deliver on its promises of democracy.

Martin was born and raised in Atlanta, Georgia. His favorite dessert was pecan pie, which is still a staple of Southern comfort food today.

Martin Luther King, Jr.
Year: 1963

Martin gave thousands of speeches in his lifetime, and to keep going he often ate foods that nourished his soul.

Martin Luther King, Jr.'s favorite: pecan pie

Serves 8

- 1 ready-to-bake pie crust
- 4¾ cups (600 g) pecan halves
- ¾ cup (165 g) light brown sugar
- 1 tablespoon all-purpose flour
- ¼ cup (55 g) butter
- 3 large eggs, lightly beaten
- 1¼ cups (390 g) golden syrup
- 1 teaspoon vanilla extract
- 3 tablespoons light cream

- Preheat the oven to 425°F (220°C) and grease a 9-inch (23-cm) pie plate. On a lightly floured surface, unroll one pie crust. Press it into the pie plate, trim the edges, then chill.

- Scatter the pecans on a chopping board and chop half of them.

- Mix the sugar and flour. Warm the butter over low heat, stirring occasionally with a wooden spoon. Take it off the heat once it has melted. Gradually stir in the sugar mixture. Beat in the eggs a little at a time, then add the golden syrup, vanilla extract, cream, and chopped pecans.

- Pour the filling mixture into the pie plate and arrange the remaining pecans on top. Bake for 5 minutes, then lower the heat to 350°F (175°C) and bake for another 20 minutes, or until just set.

- Serve warm—it's delicious with whipped cream!

September

In Atlanta, Georgia, Robert and James looked on proudly as the kitchen door at Paschal's Restaurant swung to and fro.

Waiters brought baskets of fried chicken to tables, releasing delicious smells across the dining room. In one leather booth, Martin Luther King, Jr., huddled with a group of fellow civil rights campaigners, strategizing over plates of fried chicken and mac and cheese; in another, over a peach cobbler, a group of young activists planned a protest that could change the world. The soul food diner provided a safe space for the Black community and supported those fighting for racial justice.

Robert Paschal and James Paschal
Year: 1963

Paschal's became the unofficial headquarters of the civil rights movement, and it was one of the first restaurants to seat Black and white customers at the same table in an era of segregated seating.

WE DEMAND EQUAL RIGHTS NOW!

James and Robert paid money to release arrested protesters and kept the restaurant open after normal working hours to serve them free meals.

Paschal's fried chicken
Serves 4

- 1 teaspoon white pepper
- 1 teaspoon cayenne powder
- 2 teaspoons garlic powder
- 2 teaspoons smoked paprika
- 2 teaspoons onion powder
- 2 cups (480 ml) buttermilk

- 1 tablespoon salt
- 8 boneless and skinless chicken thighs
- 4 cups (560 g) all-purpose flour
- 3 cups (710 ml) canola oil
- salt, for seasoning

- Mix the white pepper, cayenne powder, 1 teaspoon garlic powder, 1 teaspoon smoked paprika, and 1 teaspoon onion powder in a small bowl.

- Whisk the buttermilk and salt in a bowl, then stir in the seasoning mix. Add the chicken, then toss to coat. Transfer it all to a freezer bag. Refrigerate for 4 hours or overnight.

- Whisk the flour with the remaining garlic powder, paprika, and onion powder. Take your chicken out of the refrigerator and coat it in the flour mixture.

- Heat a 4-inch (10-cm) depth of oil in a shallow saucepan or deep-fat fryer until it reaches 350°F (175°C). Carefully lower in one chicken thigh at a time and fry undisturbed for 3 minutes. Flip the thigh, then fry for another 3 minutes until golden and crisp on both sides. Transfer to a tray lined with paper towels to drain. Keep warm in the oven.

- Sprinkle with salt to serve.

A wave of quiet fell across the stadium as American sprinters Tommie and John stood on the podium at the Summer Olympics in Mexico City.

After their epic performance in the 200-meter sprint, and just before the national anthem began to play, gold-winning Tommie and bronze-winning John bowed their heads and raised black-gloved fists in the air. Their silent protest was a demand for freedom and for human rights for Black people worldwide. It became an iconic image overnight, and came to represent solidarity and strength.

The raised, clenched fist, also known as the Black Power salute, is a symbol associated with Black pride.

Tommie Smith and John Carlos
Year: 1968

Tommie and John wore black socks with no shoes to highlight Black poverty. Tommie also had a scarf around his neck for Black pride, and John wore beads to pay respect to those who died as a result of slavery.

The Black Power Salute's Olympic gold cookies

Serves 18

- 1 cup (225 g) butter, softened
- 1 cup (220 g) light brown sugar
- 1 cup (200 g) superfine sugar
- 2 large eggs
- ½ teaspoon vanilla extract
- 1¼ cups (175 g) all purpose flour
- 1 teaspoon baking soda
- 1 teaspoon baking powder
- ¾ cup (75 g) flaxseed
- ½ teaspoon salt
- 3 cups (270 g) rolled oats
- 1¼ cups (160 g) dried cranberries
- 1⅓ cups (200 g) chopped walnuts
- 1 cup (170 g) chocolate chips

- Preheat oven to 350°F (175°C).

- In a large bowl, cream together the butter and both sugars until light and fluffy. Add the eggs one at a time, beating well with each addition, then stir in the vanilla.

- In a separate bowl, mix together the flour, baking soda, baking powder, flaxseed, and salt, then stir into the creamed mixture.

- Finally, stir in the oats, cranberries, walnuts, and chocolate chips.

- Drop the cookie dough onto a greased cookie sheet 1 tablespoon at a time. Wet your hands and flatten the cookies slightly.

- Bake for 15 minutes, or until golden brown.

- Let cool for 5 minutes, then place them on a wire rack. These cookies are a great source of energy and are delicious with milk!

Denison's community began preparing for Christmas on a cold November day in Greenville, North Carolina.

Due to segregation laws in the 1960s, many Greenville businesses refused to hire Black employees during the festive season. So, in response, Black people refused to purchase their gifts and food from those businesses. Boycotting these shops meant that families baked their own desserts instead, including the classic Southern banana pudding. The Black community, which made up over 30 percent of the town, also decided not to put up Christmas tree lights and decorations in their homes as a silent protest against racism.

Led by Denison, the "Christmas Sacrifice," as it became known, was the first organized demonstration by Black people in Greenville.

BLACK & WHITE CHRISTMAS!

DON'T BUY WHERE YOU CAN'T WORK!

DON'T BUY!

WE'RE DREAMING -OF- A BLACK & WHITE CHRISTMAS

The Christmas Sacrifice protest was very successful. The following year saw a large number of Black employees hired for the Christmas season.

Denison Dover Garrett
Year: 1963

The Christmas Sacrifice's banana pudding

Serves 8

- ½ cup (70 g) all-purpose flour
- pinch of salt
- 3 cups (675 ml) milk
- 1 cup (200 g) superfine sugar
- 4 large egg yolks
- ¼ cup (55 g) butter

- 2 teaspoons vanilla extract
- 12 ounces (300 g) ladyfingers
- 4 bananas, sliced
- 2 cups (235 ml) heavy cream
- ½ cup (50 g) powdered sugar

- In a non-stick pan, whisk together the flour, salt, milk, superfine sugar, and egg yolks over medium heat.

- Add in the butter and vanilla extract and whisk until everything is mixed together.

- In a large glass bowl, place an even layer of ladyfingers. Layer with a handful of sliced bananas, then pour a ladle of pudding on top. Repeat twice, making sure you leave a few ladyfingers and bananas for decoration.

- Whisk together the cream and powdered sugar to create whipped cream. Pile the whipped cream on top, decorating with your remaining bananas and ladyfingers.

- Refrigerate for a little over an hour.

- Serve immediately or refrigerate until ready to eat.

December

Georgia was working as a cook in Montgomery, Alabama, on December 1, 1955, when Rosa Parks was arrested.

Rosa was coming home from work on a busy bus when a white passenger got on. According to the law at the time, Rosa had to give up her seat, but she refused and was sent to jail. Many people supported Rosa and stopped taking the bus, known as the Montgomery Bus Boycott. For 381 days, Georgia sold homemade pies and baked goods in support of the boycott, including her famous pound cake.

Georgia Gilmore
Years: 1955–56

Georgia's food fed those who refused to ride on buses in protest. The money raised helped transport people in cars to and from work instead.

The Montgomery Bus Boycott brought about change. In November 1956, segregated seating laws came to an end and Black people could sit wherever they wanted on the bus.

The Montgomery Bus Boycott's pound cake

Serves 16

For the cake:
- 2 cups (450 g) butter, softened
- 2 cups (400 g) superfine sugar
- 5 large eggs, at room temperature, lightly beaten
- 2 teaspoons vanilla extract
- 6 tablespoons (90 ml) milk
- 2 cups (280 g) all-purpose flour

For the glaze:
- ½ cup (65 g) powdered sugar
- 3 tablespoons (45 ml) heavy cream
- ½ teaspoon vanilla extract

- Preheat the oven to 350°F (175°C) and grease a Bundt pan. In a large bowl, beat together the butter and superfine sugar with a hand mixer for 5 minutes, or until light and fluffy.

- Mix in the beaten eggs gradually, then stir in the vanilla extract and milk. Finally, sift in the flour and mix.

- Pour the batter into the pan and spread evenly. Bake for an hour.

- Once out of the oven, leave it to cool and make the glaze. Combine the powdered sugar, cream, and vanilla extract.

- Transfer the cake to a plate and drizzle the glaze over it. Cut and enjoy!

A Closer Look

Do you recognize any of the people in this book?
Learn more about them and their important work below.

Harriet Tubman
c. 1820–1913

Harriet Tubman was born into slavery on a plantation in Dorchester County, Maryland. Around her late twenties, she escaped, freeing herself before returning to liberate enslaved African Americans. Harriet sacrificed so much of her life for others; she was a spy during the Civil War, and promoted women's rights.

Robert Paschal
1909–1997

Restaurateur Robert Paschal was born in Thomson, Georgia. In 1947, he relocated to Atlanta with his brother, James, and set up a sandwich business. In 1959, they opened Paschal's Restaurant & Coffee Shop, which served as an unofficial headquarters for the civil rights movement and earned a reputation as Atlanta's "Black City Hall."

Denison Dover Garrett
1915–2011

Denison Dover Garrett was born in Pitt County, North Carolina. After his family lost their farm, they moved to Greenville, where he later became the council's first Black candidate. Denison led the county's NAACP (National Association for the Advancement of Colored People) branch and organized the 1963 Christmas Sacrifice.

Georgia Gilmore
1920–1990

Georgia Gilmore was born in Montgomery, Alabama, and was working as a cook when the bus boycott began in 1955. After civil rights activist Rosa Parks was arrested for refusing to give up her seat on the bus to a white passenger, Georgia organized a group of bakers and cooks to fundraise to sustain the 381-day boycott.

James Paschal
1920–2008

Chef James Paschal was born in Thomson, Georgia, as the younger brother of Robert. In 1959, they opened Paschal's Restaurant & Coffee Shop, where their fried chicken was extremely popular. Martin Luther King, Jr., and other civil rights leaders held strategy meetings at the restaurant, and families and friends would reunite there after protests.

Leah Chase
1923–2019

Leah Chase was born in New Orleans, Louisiana, the home of Creole cooking. At 22 years old, Leah married Edgar "Dooky" Chase II, whose parents owned the Dooky Chase Restaurant. Leah became a chef, later known as the "Queen of Creole Cuisine," and fed the Freedom Riders, along with many other civil rights activists, including Martin Luther King, Jr.

Hosea Williams
1926–2000

Born in Attapulgus, Georgia, Hosea Williams became a civil rights activist after being attacked for drinking from a "Whites Only" water fountain. He became one of the most trusted advisors of Martin Luther King, Jr., and played an important role in the 1965 Selma to Montgomery marches for fair voting rights.

Opal Lee
b. 1926

Born in Marshall, Texas, Opal Lee was 12 years old when, on one Juneteenth day, arsonists burned down her home in a racist attack. Opal spent the rest of her life campaigning for equality and justice, and took a symbolic walk from Fort Worth, Texas, to Washington, D.C., to gain national recognition for Juneteenth.

Martin Luther King, Jr.
1929–1968

Born in Atlanta, Georgia, Martin Luther King, Jr., first experienced segregation at 6 years old, when a white friend was no longer allowed to play with him. Martin became a believer in peaceful protest, inspired by the Indian activist Mahatma Gandhi. A year after his "I Have a Dream" speech, Martin became the youngest man to receive the Nobel Peace Prize.

Bobby Seale
b. 1936

Born in Dallas, Texas, Bobby Seale moved to California as a young adult and met civil rights activist Huey P. Newton. They launched the Black Panther Party, which was active from 1966 to 1982. It was formed to challenge police brutality, but from 1969 onward, its focus turned to food injustice.

John Lewis
1940–2020

John Lewis was born near Troy, Alabama, and grew up on a farm where his parents were sharecroppers (people who farm a piece of land owned by someone else). John led the 1965 Selma to Montgomery marches to protect the Black American's right to vote, and later served for thirty-three years in the United States House of Representatives.

David Richmond
1941–1990

Born in Greensboro, North Carolina, David Richmond met Franklin McCain, Ezell Blair, Jr., and Joseph McNeil at North Carolina Agricultural and Technical State University. In 1960, they sat at a "Whites Only" restaurant counter and returned for the next five days with more students. These protests, known as the Greensboro sit-ins, led to the desegregation of restaurants.

Franklin McCain
1941–2014

Franklin McCain was born in Union County, North Carolina. He grew up in Washington, D.C., but returned to his home state to attend North Carolina Agricultural and Technical State University. He was one of the original Greensboro Four, and once said he sees freedom as the ability to "be oneself in society at large."

Ezell Blair, Jr.
b. 1941

Ezell Blair, Jr., was born in Greensboro, North Carolina. His father was an NAACP member who often spoke on the subject of racial injustices. Ezell was one of the original Greensboro Four, and would later become president of his school's student government association, the campus NAACP, and the Greensboro Congress for Racial Equality.

Huey P. Newton
1942–1989

Huey P. Newton was born in Monroe, Louisiana, but moved to Oakland, California, during World War II. He met civil rights activist Bobby Seale at college, and together they set up the Black Panther Party as a response to their strong belief that the civil rights movement had failed to improve the treatment of Black Americans.

Joseph McNeil
b. 1942

Joseph McNeil was born in Wilmington, North Carolina, and fought against segregation in the South. He was one of the original Greensboro Four, and after staging the sit-ins, McNeil became involved with the formation of the Student Executive Committee for Justice, a student group created in response to the sit-ins.

Tommie Smith
b. 1944

Born in Clarksville, Texas, Tommie Smith earned a spot on the US National Track and Field team for the 1968 Olympics in Mexico City, where he became the first person in history to run the 200-meter race in under twenty seconds. During the medals ceremony, he and fellow athlete John Carlos each held a fist in the air as a display of solidarity for human rights for Black people.

John Carlos
b. 1945

Born in Harlem, New York, John Carlos was a gifted track-and-field athlete. Along with Tommie Smith, John earned a spot on the US National Track and Field team for the 1968 Olympics in Mexico City, and came in third in the 200-meter race. Standing on the podium, Tommie and John raised their fists in a Black Power salute. They were suspended from the team and the Olympic Village for their actions.

Rob Rubba
b. 1979

Born in New Jersey, Rob Rubba was studying fine arts in college when he discovered his passion for pastry. He enrolled in culinary school and was running a pop-up restaurant in Washington, D.C., when he decided to put his artistic talents to good use: creating the graphics for the Bakers Against Racism social media accounts.

Paola Velez
b. 1990

Born to parents from the Dominican Republic, chef Paola Velez was working at a donut pop-up in Washington, D.C., during the 2020 Black Lives Matter protests in the wake of police officer Derek Chauvin killing George Floyd. Paola conceptualized and organized Bakers Against Racism, a global virtual bake sale which raised over a million dollars.

Willa Lou Pelini
b. 1994

Born in Minneapolis, Minnesota, Willa Lou Pelini was working as a pastry chef in Washington, D.C., when fellow chef Paola Velez came to her with the idea for Bakers Against Racism. Willa was aiming for eighty people to join in their bake sale, but instead they sparked a global movement that ignited solidarity for racial justice on five continents.

Glossary

activist a person who campaigns to bring about change

boycott a movement or action in which people refuse to buy a product or take part in an activity as a way of expressing strong disapproval

campaign a planned set of activities that people carry out in order to achieve something, such as political change

civil rights the rights that people have in a society to equal treatment and equal social opportunities, regardless of their race, religion, gender, sexual identity, disability, age, or other personal characteristics

democracy a government that is run by the people

demonstration a march or gathering that people take part in to show they are against something or they support something

Emancipation Proclamation the proclamation issued by President Abraham Lincoln on January 1, 1863, that enslaved people in Confederate states were "forever free"

Freedom Rider someone who participated in Freedom Rides, bus trips through the American South in 1961 to protest segregated seating in interstate buses and terminals

human rights the basic rights and freedoms that belong to every person

inequality occurs when things are not equal

justice fairness in the way that people are treated

plantation a large farm producing crops like cotton or sugar that historically depended on the labor of enslaved people

protest the act of saying or showing that you object to something

racism the harmful belief that one race is better than another, and the behavior driven by this belief

rebellion the act of not following the government's laws

segregation the division of groups of people by keeping them physically apart from each other

sit-in a form of protest in which people occupy a space and refuse to leave until their demands are met

slavery when a person is treated as the property of another person

solidarity unity within a group

Underground Railroad a network of routes, places, and supporters who helped enslaved people in the American South escape to the North

Further Reading

The ABCs of Black History
by Rio Cortez and illustrated by Lauren Semmer

Civil Rights Stories: Racial Equality
by Anita Ganeri and illustrated by Toby Newsome

Civil Rights Stories: Slavery
by Catherine Chambers and illustrated by Toby Newsome

The Juneteenth Story: Celebrating the End of Slavery in the United States
by Alliah L. Agostini and illustrated by Sawyer Cloud

Little People, Big Dreams: Harriet Tubman
by Maria Isabel Sánchez Vegara and illustrated by Pili Aguado

Little People, Big Dreams: Martin Luther King, Jr.
by Maria Isabel Sánchez Vegara and illustrated by Mai Ly Degnan

Opal Lee and What It Means to Be Free: The True Story of the Grandmother of Juneteenth
by Alice Faye Duncan and illustrated by Keturah A. Bobo

Pies from Nowhere: How Georgia Gilmore Sustained the Montgomery Bus Boycott
by Dee Romito and illustrated by Laura Freeman

Timelines from Black History: Leaders, Legends, Legacies
by DK